(11) What happened while Pe

MW00717084

_____

(12) What was unusual about that?

_____

Until his vision, Peter had believed that the blessings of God were for the Jews alone. However, when he heard these men speaking in tongues and magnifying God, he became totally convinced that God wanted to make Himself known to the Gentiles as well.

Discussion Question: Can you share a time God has changed your preconceived ideas about Him?

(13) What did Peter say?

_____

_____

_____

Read **Acts 11:1–18.**
(14) What happened when Peter came to Jerusalem?

_____

(15) Why?

_____

(16) What happened after he had made his explanation?

_____

_____

Peter's argument that God had blessed the Gentiles with the gift of the Spirit in exactly the same way that He had blessed the Jewish believers on the Day of Pentecost and that they had also spoken in tongues was sufficient to convince the Jewish believers.

Read **Acts 19:1-7.**
(17) Where did this account take place?

_____

(18) What question did Paul ask?

_____

_____

(19) What was their answer?

_____

(20) What happened when Paul baptized these people in water and laid hands upon them?

_____

_____

We have seen in these three instances that the baptism in the Spirit is a concise, definite, instantaneous happening. In each of these occasions the one factor which is consistent is that *all* the recipients on *all* the occasions, were said to speak in tongues as a direct result of having been filled with the Spirit. We, therefore, suggest that speaking in tongues is a genuine and reliable initial evidence of receiving the Spirit.

There are two other accounts in *Acts* of believers receiving the Spirit.

Read Acts 8.
(21) To where did Philip travel during the persecution?

_____

(22) What was the people's attitude to Philip's preaching?

_____

(23) What was their response to the signs Philip performed?

_____

(24) What was the result (v. 12)?

_____

(25) What happened when Peter and John laid hands on them?

_____

Although this account does not specifically say that the new Christians spoke in tongues, Simon, the magician, saw something happen as a direct result of their receiving the Spirit. Whatever it was, it occurred suddenly, dramatically and in a visible way. Simon desired the ability to make this phenomenon happen. Is it not feasible to assume that he saw the same sign that had occurred on the other occasions?

Read **Acts 9:1–19.**

This is the dramatic story of Saul's (Paul) of Tarsus conversion.

(26) What did Ananias minister to Paul (v. 17)?

_____

In this immediate context, the Scripture does not say Paul spoke in tongues, but we know that later it was common for him to do so.

Read **1 Corinthians 14:18.**

(27) Although Paul was writing to the Corinthians to correct a misuse of tongues' speaking, what does he say?

_____

Read **1 Corinthians 14:5, 39.**

(28) What else does he say concerning tongues?

_____

_____

On the basis of the foregoing evidence of Biblical experience, we humbly affirm that speaking in tongues is the first scriptural evidence of the baptism in the Spirit. We also affirm that there are many other scriptural evidences which should follow this without which the experience is incomplete.

Personal Application:

(1) Am I willing to accept speaking in tongues as the initial evidence of the baptism in the Holy Spirit for today as well as in the Early Church?

(2) Am I willing to put behind me any misgivings I have about the scriptural basis of speaking in tongues?

(3) Am I willing to ask God for this experience?

Memory Work

"Suddenly there came a sound from heaven as of a rushing mighty wind, and it filled all the house where they were sitting. And there appeared unto them cloven tongues like as of fire and it sat upon each of them. And they were all filled with the Holy Spirit and began to speak with other tongues, as the Spirit gave them utterance" (Acts 2:2-4).

The Holy Spirit and the Believer

Introduction

Before He died, Jesus told His sorrowing disciples that it was to their advantage that He go away because when He did, He would send the Holy Spirit. As long as Jesus was on earth, He was limited by what He could do physically in a certain time period. The Holy Spirit, on the other hand, is limited only by the human will.

The first goal of the Spirit in our life is to produce salvation. Once we are saved, He turns His efforts toward giving us power for holy living and service.

Prayer: Lord, please forgive me for not understanding the importance of the Holy Spirit's work in me. I want to learn everything You have to teach me. Amen.

Bible Study

Read **John 16:8-11.**

(1) What did Jesus say the Holy Spirit would do when He came?

_____

(2) Why for sin?

_____

(3) Why for righteousness?

_____

(4) Why for judgment?

_____

An important aspect of the Holy Spirit's work is to convict, reprove and convince unconverted people about sin, righteousness and judgment. Without the Spirit's work of conviction, we would remain ignorant of our sinful and lost condition. The Holy Spirit makes us aware of the sinfulness of sin, how far short we come of God's standard of righeousness, and of the awful judgment which awaits every sinner.

Discussion Question: Share a time when you were very much aware of the Spirit's conviction or reproval.

The Holy Spirit also brings conversion and regeneration.

Read **Titus 3:4-6.**
(5) Why did God save according to this verse?

_____

(6) What was it not on account of?

_____

(7) How did He save us?

_____

(8) How was the Holy Spirit given to us?

_____

Read **Ephesians 2:1.**
(9) What does God, through His Holy Spirit, do?

_____

_____

Before we know Jesus, we are spiritually dead. When we accept Him, we also receive the Holy Spirit, who gives life to our dead spirits. The Day of Pentecost marked the beginning of the Age of the Holy Spirit. Now God would perform His work among men through the Holy Spirit.

Read **John 3:5,6.**
(10) During His earthly ministry Jesus repeatedly announced the ushering in of the kingdom of heaven. What is the essential requirement of this kingdom?

_____

Read **Romans 8:2.**
(11) What does Paul say the law of the Spirit of life in Jesus has done for him?

_____

J.B. Phillips translates this verse from *Romans* as "The new spiritual principle of life in Christ Jesus lifts me out of the old vicious circle of sin and death."

Read **Romans 8:16** and **1 John 5:6.**

(12) How does the Spirit give assurance of our salvation?

_____

Think how gracious God is. Not only does He make us His children when we become saved, but He gives the additional assurance of the witness of His Holy Spirit.

Discussion Question: Can you share a time when the Holy Spirit has given you needed assurance about your salvation?

Read **John 16:13.**

(13) What is another aspect of the Holy Spirit's ministry?

_____

(14) How does He do this?

_____

Read **John 14:16,17,26.**

(15) What does Jesus call the Holy Spirit here?

_____

Discussion Question: _Another_ Comforter implies that there had been a first comforter or helper, as the word is frequently translated. Who was the first Comforter?

When Jesus spoke of the coming of the Holy Spirit, He was preparing His disciples for His departure. They, of course, were appalled at the thought that He was going to leave them.

(16) What reassurance about the Comforter did He give them?

_____

In essence, Jesus told His disciples that, although He must leave them physically, the Father was going to send Someone else to take His place, Someone who would never leave them.

(17) What else would He do?

_____

Read **Romans 8:11.**

(18) Give another aspect of the Holy Spirit's work.

_____

The word *mortal* means *bound to die* and refers to our physical bodies. The word *quicken* means to *impart life.* Therefore, the promise of this scripture is that the Holy Spirit, when He dwells within us, will impart life, strength, health and vigor to our bodies. Living in the Spirit is a health-promoting exercise. It will increase our physical strength and our life span.

Read **Acts 1:8.**

(19) In telling the disciples to stay in Jerusalem until they had received the Holy Spirit, what did Jesus say would happen?

_____

(20) What would this power enable them to do?

_____

Jesus used the word *dunamis* from which we derive our word *dynamo,* a machine which self-generates a consistent and continuing supply of power. Thus the power of the Spirit within us generates power to enable us to witness of Christ. Not only are we enabled to bear witness of Jesus, we actually become witness to Him.

Another very important aspect of the Holy Spirit's ministry is His empowering of our prayers.

Read **Ephesians 6:18** and **Jude 20.**

(21) What are we commanded to do in these verses?

_____

Discussion Question: What do you think praying in the Spirit means?

Read **Romans 8:26,27** in the NIV Bible.

(22) Why do we need the Holy Spirit's help when we pray?

_____

(23) How does He intercede for us?

_____

Sometimes when we pray in the Spirit, words are no longer adequate and we find ourselves actually groaning in prayer. This is the Holy Spirit praying through us "with groans that words cannot express."

(24) What is the advantage of having the Holy Spirit intercede for us?

_____

When we pray, we cannot always be sure that we are praying in the will of God, but, when we pray in the Spirit, we pray the perfect prayer because the Holy Spirit has the mind of God.

Another way the Holy Spirit helps us is in our *worship*.

Read **Acts 2:1-11.**
(25) When the people gathered in Jerusalem heard the disciples speaking in other tongues, what amazed them most?

_____

_____

(26) What were the disciples saying?

_____

Read **Acts 10:44-46.**
(27) What were the men speaking in tongues doing?

_____

The Holy Spirit inspires a continual praise and worship of God in us once we have been baptized in the Holy Spirit. Many times when we are praying in our tongue or singing, we will have the sense of worshiping and glorifying God.

Read **John 4:24.**
(28) What two ways must we worship God?

_____

How do we worship God in spirit? Men have often debated this question. But by the giving of the Holy Spirit, we can now worship God in our spirits, which are joined to the Holy Spirit.

Read **Philippians 3:3.**
(29) Who does Paul say are of the *true* circumsion (God's inheritors)?

_____

_____

Read **Galatians 5:22,23.**
(30) What is the fruit of the Spirit?

_____

The fruit of the Spirit cannot be produced by the natural man. No matter how refined or educated a person may be, God's character is only seen in him when God the Holy Spirit lives in him.

Personal Application:

(1) Are there things I'm doing that I know hinder the work of the Holy Spirit?
(2) Am I truly willing to cooperate with Him and the work He is doing in me?

Receiving the Holy Spirit

If you answered yes to Questions 1 and 2, you are now ready to receive the fullness of the Spirit.

The first qualification to be a candidate for the baptism in the Spirit is that you must have received Jesus Christ as your Savior. If you are a child of God, then you may receive the gifts of the Holy Spirit. The second requirement is that you must deeply desire this blessing. Jesus expressed it this way, *"If any man thirst, let him come unto me and drink" (John 7:37)*. Are you thirsty for the water of the Spirit? If you are, then you may come to Jesus and drink. It is as simple as that.

Remember that you do not have to earn this blessing. If you did, it would no longer be the *gift* of the Holy Spirit. You can never earn or merit this wonderful blessing, nor do you have to. It is yours as a free gift. I would like to suggest three simple little words which could enable you to receive this precious blessing. The words are *relax, receive, respond.* Let us look at them briefly.

1. *Relax* Relax physically first and this will help you relax spiritually and emotionally. Why not sit down somewhere comfortably. The disciples were actually sitting on the day of Pentecost, so this is a good scriptural posture for receiving the Spirit. Sit back and relax. You are in good hands—the hands of Jesus. He is the Baptizer in the Holy Spirit.

2. *Receive* It would be good right now for you to ask Jesus to baptize you in the Spirit. Ask simply, quietly and in faith. Do not begin to beg or plead. You do not have to shout or moan. Jesus is right with you. He can hear your prayer. When you have quietly asked Him to fill you with the Spirit, then in faith, you must believe that He has answered your prayer and receive the Spirit by faith.

Remember that the word for spirit is also the same word for breath. Why not just open your mouth, take a deep breath, and breathe in the Holy Spirit? This is what Jesus referred to as drinking of the Spirit. Just as you open your mouth to drink water, you can also open your mouth to drink in the Spirit. Open your mouth and breathe in and, as you do, believe that the Holy Spirit is coming into your life in a new way. Do it in faith. *"What things soever you desire, when you pray, believe that you receive them, and you shall have them" (Mark 11:24).*

You are doing this by faith. Remember, it is not feelings. You may not feel any emotional response. This is not an emotional experience. It is a spiritual experience. There may or may not be an emotional accompaniment. If there is, relax and enjoy it. If there is not, then do not worry about it. Emotions are very erratic and unreliable. The important thing is not what you feel. It is what you believe. Believe that you have received the Spirit. This is the first step, then: "breathing in" the Holy Spirit. As you do it, begin to give joyful thanks and praise to God for filling you with the Spirit. Let your heart begin to reach out to God in praise and keep drinking ever more deeply of the Spirit.

3. *Respond* Now we come to the third step, your response to the Spirit, who is now beginning to fill your whole being. Having breathed in, you must also breathe out. You breathe in the Spirit; now you must breathe out praise to God, in faith for His blessing. When you do this, do not speak in your own native tongue. Aspire to praise God, but believe to do it in a new language which the Spirit will give you.

Speaking in tongues is a miracle. It is a supernatural ability given by the Spirit. This does not mean that it is difficult to do. It simply means that you must cooperate with God. This is well illustrated by the story of Peter walking on the water (Matt. 14:29). Jesus called out to Peter, *"Come,"* and then we read, *"And when Peter was come down out of the ship, he walked on the water, to go to Jesus."* When Peter walked on the water, he was not consciously doing anything supernatural. He was walking just as naturally as though he were on solid ground. The miracle was that he did not sink! It is like this when we begin to speak in tongues. We use our tongue and lips in just the same way we do when we speak in our native language. The miracle is not in the physical act of speaking. The miracle is in the language that we are given to speak. In other words, it is not how you speak, but what you speak, that is a miracle. Speaking is a natural act, just as walking is.

When you speak in tongues, the physical part of it is just as natural as any other time you exercise your powers of speech. The miracle occurs when the Holy Spirit gives you words to speak in a language which you have never learned or possibly even heard before. I must emphasize this matter of the simplicity of speaking in tongues. So many people have a problem at this point; they make it hard for themselves. They believe that it is too difficult for them to do. Some become tense instead of nicely relaxed. Many people are so sincere in their desire that it will not be themselves speaking that they sit woodenly inactive, waiting for God to take over their vocal cords and speak through their lips, without their playing any active part. Please notice in Acts 2:4 that *"They"*—the disciples—are the subject of the sentence. It was, therefore, the disciples who were all filled with the

Holy Spirit, and they, the disciples, who *"began to speak with other tongues, as the Spirit gave them utterance."* They began to speak.

When you begin to speak in tongues, it will be *you* who will initiate it. You will speak the words, but the Holy Spirit will give them to you. The Holy Spirit will furnish you with sounds, words, phrases in your mind. These will sound very strange to you. It is a language which you have never heard before, very probably an angelic or heavenly language, which sounds very different from any earthly language that you know. As the Spirit gives you these words in your mind, speak them out. Speak them forth boldly. Do not be afraid. Initially, you may only have one or two words. You may find yourself repeating them over and over. Just do that.

As you speak them out boldly in faith, the Holy Spirit will increase your vocabulary. The flow of words will increase until rivers begin to flow forth from your innermost being. Determine, therefore, that when you have breathed in the Holy Spirit, you will follow that by breathing out praise to God. Determine to do it with your voice, but not with your native language. Speak out forcefully whatever the Spirit puts into your mind. You may sense your lips beginning to tremble and feel that your mouth is full of strange sounds. Speak them out boldly.

Once you begin to speak, keep it up. Do not stop. Let it keep flowing. The more it flows, the freer you will become. Do not worry what it sounds like; that is the Holy Spirit's business. He will give the particular language He desires you to have at this time. As you continue to exercise this gift of tongues, you go from language to language, for there are different kinds of tongues (1 Cor. 12:10). Once you have spoken in tongues, as the Spirit gives you utterance, you can exercise this gift whenever you wish. It will depend on your decision and initiative. Paul says, *"What is it then, I will pray with the spirit, and I will pray with the understanding" (1 Cor. 14:15).*

Whether with the understanding, or with the Spirit, you pray when you will. Exercise this ability every day and several times each day. Whenever you do, it will strengthen and bless you, for Paul tells us *"He that speaketh in an unknown tongue edifieth himself" (1 Cor. 14:4).* You build yourself up spiritually every time you speak and pray in a new language. This is one gift of the Spirit which edifies the one who exercises it.

Memory Work

"The Spirit Himself bears witness with our spirit that we are children of God" (Rom. 8:16).
"And in the same way the Spirit also helps our weakness; for we do not know how to pray as we should, but the Spirit Himself intercedes for us with groanings too deep for words" (Rom. 8:26).

27

Why Speak in Tongues?

Introduction

Few subjects have suffered as much misunderstanding as speaking in tongues has. In this lesson, we are going to find the answer to a question many people have asked: What is the purpose or benefit of speaking in languages which one does not understand?

Prayer: Lord, I know You give only good gifts. Help me to understand what You hope to achieve in me when You give me the gift of tongues. Thank You, Jesus.

Bible Study

People who would put down God's gift of speaking in tongues frequently use some of Paul's statements which were specifically directed against the more unruly members of the Corinthian church. However, Paul made other statements that show how he felt about this gift.

Read **1 Corinthians 14:5.**
(1) What does Paul say in this verse?

_____

Read **1 Corinthians 14:18.**
(2) What does Paul say here?

_____

Notice Paul's intimate emphasis, *"I thank my God..."* Speaking to God in languages of the Spirit increases and strengthens the awareness of one's personal, intimate relationship and fellowship with God.

Discussion Question: Have you personally experienced this intimate fellowship with God? Share an experience that was particularly meaningful to you.

Read **1 Corinthians 14:2.**
(3) What does Paul call speaking in tongues in this verse?

_____

Paul thanked God for the privilege of speaking such sacred and intimate mysteries.

Read **1 Corinthians 14:14.**
(4) What does Paul say about our understanding when we pray in tongues?

_____

When Paul says our understanding is unfruitful, he means that our mind is in neutral. Thus we are relaxed, refreshed and edified by this spiritual exercise.

What is God's purpose in giving us a language we don't understand.

The first reason for speaking in tongues is that it is God's will for us.

Discussion Questions: Do you believe God wants every Christian to speak in tongues? If not, why not?

Read **Acts 2:4.**

This is the scene in Jerusalem when on the Day of Pentecost the Holy Spirit fell on the disciples.

(5) What was the physical evidence of their infilling with the Holy Spirit?

_____

Read **Acts 10:46.**

When Peter visited the house of Cornelius, the Roman centurion, and shared the Gospel with the people there, much the same thing happened, amazing Peter's Jewish companions.

(6) What does Scripture say happened which startled the Jewish converts?

_____

The source of their amazement lay in the fact that till this time, these people had believed that the baptism in the Holy Spirit was for Jewish converts only.

Read **Acts 19:6.**

When Paul was in Ephesus, he came upon a group of believers who knew nothing about the Holy Spirit.

(7) When he laid hands upon them, what was the result?

_____

_____

The second reason for speaking in tongues is that it is the scriptural, initial evidence of the fullness of the Spirit.

Read **Romans 8:26,27.**
(8) What problem does Paul make note of here?

_____

This is one of our human weaknesses. Sometimes when we go to pray, we are conscious that we need help and assistance, but we don't understand what is really wrong nor how to pray about it.

(9) How does the Spirit overcome this inadequacy for us?

_____

(10) How is He able to do this?

_____

Because the Holy Spirit is God, He is able to search our heart and discover just where we are and what is amiss.

(11) What does the Holy Spirit know?

_____

Knowing the mind of the Spirit is another way of saying that the Holy Spirit knows God's will for us.

(12) How does the Spirit pray?

_____

By praying according to the will of God, the Holy Spirit brings us into harmony with that will. He prays out all the complexes, inhibitions, negative thoughts which have hindered us, and He prays us into the positive, powerful, beneficial purpose of God for our life. This kind of praying is one of the most powerful means of "renewing the spirit of our mind."

The third reason for speaking in tongues is that it is a therapeutic means of cleansing and release.

Praying for others particularly our loved ones can sometimes be difficult for us as well. When we know people have a problem or when God puts someone on our heart to pray for, we don't always know how to pray for them. Our feelings for them and our lack of knowledge concerning God's will for them can both be hindrances.

How do we pray for others at times such as these? The answer is *in tongues.*

The fourth reason for praying in tongues is that it enables us to pray perfect prayers either for ourselves or others.

Discussion Question: Can you relate an experience or a time when you did not know how to pray for someone and what happened?

Reread **1 Corinthians 14:4.**
(13) What does this verse say is one of the benefits of praying in tongues?

_____

It is from the word *edify* that we derive our word *edifice* or *building.* Whenever we speak in tongues, though the words may be a mystery to our intellect, we are building ourselves up spiritually.

Our fifth reason for speaking in tongues is that it is a source of personal edification.

Reread **1 Corinthians 14:2.**
(14) Who are we speaking to when we pray in our tongue?

_____

(15) Where are we speaking these "mysteries"?

_____

The primary purpose of this spiritual exercise is not that we speak to men, but rather that we may speak to God. Communing with God in this manner, we are freed from the limitations and restrictions of our puny, finite mind. We are not restricted to speaking only of those things which we have learned and imbibed in our intellect. We are released to speak also of things which we are taught intuitively by the Spirit of God. We commune with God about deep things, which remain a mystery to our finite mind.

Our sixth reason for speaking in tongues is that it is a realm of intimate spiritual communion with God.

Read **1 Corinthians 14:17,18.**

(16) What does Paul say we do when we speak in tongues?

_____

Discussion Question: Have you ever felt unable to adequately express your thanks and appreciation to God? Share an experience.

God has been so good that mere words seem too weak to express the reservoir of thanks we feel within. Then here is a fulfilling way to do it. Paul says we can "give thanks well" by speaking to God by the Spirit, in the language He gives. This giving of thanks supercedes anything that our human mind can furnish. It goes beyond the realm of poetry and ministers to God in the Spirit.

Our seventh reason for speaking in tongues is that it is an opportunity to "give thanks" acceptably to God.

Read **1 Corinthians 14:15** and **Jude 20.**

(17) What does Paul call praying in tongues in this verse?

_____

The eighth reason is it enables us to pray "in the Spirit."

Read **Isaiah 28:11,12.**

This is a prophecy of Isaiah relating to the age in which we live.

(18) How does Isaiah say God will speak to His people?

_____

(19) What does God call it?

_____

In this day of extreme stress, man perhaps needs rest more than in any other age. Communing with God in tongues is a most relaxing and refreshing experience. The body and mind can relax completely. We do not have to think what to say next or how to say it. The Spirit flows through us in perfect communion with the Father, and we receive the benefit of that beautiful communion. It is a tonic for spirit, soul and body.

The ninth reason is that it is a source of rest and refreshing.

Reread **Acts 2:11.**

(20) What amazed the Jews on the Day of Pentecost?

_____

(11) What happened while Peter was preaching?

_____

Reread **Acts 10:46.**
(21) Finish this sentence: For they heard them speak with tongues

   and _____

Very often when we speak in tongues, the Spirit is worshiping, praising and eulogizing God. The Holy Spirit is magnifying the wonderful works of God through us.

Our tenth reason is that it is a ministry of praise and worship to God.

Read **Ephesians 5:18.**
(22) What are we told to do in this verse?

_____

This verse in *The Amplified Bible* is translated: "Be...being filled." It is a grammatical form we do not have in English, which indicates a continuous action.

Our eleventh reason is that speaking in tongues is a scriptural means of maintaining the fullness of the Spirit.

Ministering to God in tongues is a valid means of keeping filled with the Spirit. Therefore, we ought to do this every day and many times each day.

Read **1 Corinthians 14:5.**
(23) What does speaking in tongues, plus interpretation, do?

_____

Our personal devotional tongue or prayer language is edifying to the one who exercises it. He alone is built up by the use of it. However, if this tongue is interpreted, it may also be a blessing to others. The one who speaks in tongues should also pray that he may interpret in order that other believers may receive edification, too.

Read **James 1:26, 3:1-18.**
(24) To what does James compare our tongue?

_____

James teaches that the tongue is the control center of a man. When we offer our control center to the Holy Spirit, He begins to bring our conversation under Christ's control. Our surrender to the Holy Spirit in the gift of tongues is a release of the sweet water of life, God's words. By regular daily use of this gift, we will find strength to resist negative and critical talk.

Read **Ephesians 4:29.**

(25) What does good conversation do?

_____

Speaking in tongues is a means of producing Christ's mind in us, so that we speak only those things that are useful to build up ourselves and our hearers. Speaking in tongues purifies and renews our mind, which is the source of our conversation and way of life.

Our twelfth reason for speaking in tongues is that it is a key to bringing in the mind of Christ over our own mind.

(26) Summarize the reasons God wants Christians to have the gift of tongues.

_____

_____

_____

_____

_____

Discussion Question: How many of these purposes have you been aware of as you have prayed? Share some experiences.

Personal Application:

(1) If you are not currently doing so, are you willing to make praying in the Spirit a regular important part of your prayer life?

(2) Praying in tongues is not primarily an emotional experience. Are you willing to be obedient to God in this way regardless of how you feel?

Memory Work

"What is it, then? I will pray with the spirit, and I will pray with the understanding also; I will sing with the spirit, and I will sing with the understanding also" (1 Cor. 14:15).

The Gifts of the Spirit

Introduction

The great spiritual revival which is sweeping the world at this time has been called the Charismatic Renewal. This phrase has been employed to describe an extremely important aspect of this revival, the restoration to the church of the supernatural manifestations which were so powerfully obvious in the New Testament Church. These manifestations, or gifts of the Spirit, have been noticeably absent from the church for many centuries. In the past 50 years, God has been restoring these features, and His restoration program has been accelerated greatly in the past 20 years. The Charismatic Renewal has invaded every part of the Christian Church, bringing new life and power to the Body of Christ. The restoration of these blessings creates a great need for teaching on these important subjects.

There are many charismatic gifts mentioned in the Bible. The main areas of reference are Romans 12:3-8, 1 Corinthians 12:8-10, 28-30, and Ephesians 4:11. For the purpose of this study, we will limit ourselves to a consideration of the nine manifestations listed in 1 Corinthians 12:8-10.

Prayer: Father, we praise You and magnify Your name. We thank You for Your marvelous gift to us—Your Holy Spirit. Teach us now, as we commit this study to You. Amen.

Bible Study

Read **1 Corinthians 12:1.**
(1) How do know God wants us to be knowledgeable about the spiritual gifts?

_____

_____

Discussion Question: Why are they called gifts?

Read **1 Corinthians 12:8-10.**
(2) What are the spiritual gifts given in this verse?

35

Read **1 Corinthians 12:4-7.**

(3) Who is the giver of these spiritual gifts?

(4) What are the gifts given for?

(5) Who may be used in this ministry?

Read **1 Corinthians 1:7.**

(6) What is Paul's concern for this church?

Read **Ephesians 5:18.**

(7) What does Paul tell the members of the Ephesian church to do?

Read **1 Corinthians 12:31** and **14:12.**

(8) What is to be our attitude toward spiritual gifts?

(9) What is one reason we should desire them?

(10) Paul's position regarding the gifts of the Spirit is crystal clear. Summarize his teaching in these first nine questions.

To simplify our study of the gifts of the Spirit, we will classify them into three categories:

GIFTS OF SPEECH	GIFTS OF REVELATION	GIFTS OF ABILITY
Tongues	Word of Wisdom	Faith
Interpretation of Tongues	Word of Knowledge	Gifts of Healings
Prophecy	Discerning of Spirits	Working of Miracles

Discussion Question: Tell about a time when one of the spiritual gifts ministered especially to you.

36

The Gift of Tongues

The manifestation of tongues has two functions: first, as "devotional tongues," the purpose of which is to edify the person using it; second, as the gift of tongues, which, when used in conjunction with the companion gift of interpretation of tongues, is for the edifying of the whole church and not merely the individual.

Because the Corinthian church in particular, and many churches since then, have abused the public ministry of the gift of tongues, it is important that we pay attention to the guidelines Paul established for the Corinthian church.

Read **1 Corinthians 13:1.**
(11) What must always be our motivation in using this gift?

_____

Read **1 Corinthians 14:5, 13, 27.**
(12) With what should it always be accompanied?

_____

(13) Is there any limitation on its use?

_____

_____

Any believer who has ever spoken in tongues is capable of edifying the Body through an utterance in tongues. You should, therefore, be prepared to do so at any time. Seek to be yielded to the Spirit. Be relaxed in your mind and be open to the Holy Spirit. Develop a sensitivity to what the Spirit is seeking to do or say in any particular service. When the Holy Spirit wants to bring a tongue utterance through you, there will generally be an inner awareness of this for some time before you actually speak. This is often a gentle stirring in your spirit, a growing excitement and anticipation. This develops into a deep awareness that the Spirit is going to bring an utterance and that this utterance is within you.

Read **1 Corinthians 14:32.**

Discussion Question: If you have ever spoken in tongues at a public meeting, share your first time of ministry.

(14) Who is in control of the actual utterance?

_____

Many people expect the Holy Spirit to take control of their mouths and do the talking. However, this scripture shows us that the person giving the utterance has control over it. The Holy Spirit gives the inspiration for it. Therefore, if the time is not right for the giving of a message in tongues, you do not have to speak out immediately. You can wait quietly for the right moment to speak. The Holy Spirit will prompt you clearly at that time. *He will not interrupt what is already happening in the service.*

Read 1 Corinthians 14:33.
(15)   How do we know that the Holy Spirit will not bring confusion to a meeting?

_____

It follows logically then that if there is confusion brought into a meeting, it comes from another source, rather than from God.

Discussion Question: Discuss any confusion you have seen at meetings and who or what you believe was responsible for it.

If you feel the Spirit has a message in tongues for you to give, remain calm and relaxed, and, when He lets you know the time is right, speak in a normal but clearly audible voice. When the utterance is complete, all must wait upon God for the interpretation. Often some other believer will be given the interpretation.

Read 1 Corinthians 14:13,16.
(16)   What do you do if no one else has the interpretation?

_____

(17)   Why?

_____

_____

The interpretation of tongues
The interpretation of tongues is the companion gift to that of tongues and is always used in conjunction with that gift. It is the supernatural enablement by the Holy Spirit to interpret an utterance in tongues into the natural language of the congregation. It is *not* the gift of translation. By this gift of the Spirit, the believer concerned is able to render the utterance intelligible to the congregation, so they may receive it and be edified by it.

Read **1 Corinthians 12:11.**
(18) Who may interpet?

Any Spirit-filled believer may be chosen and anointed by the Spirit to manifest this gift. Here again, we must seek to develop a sensitivity to the Holy Spirit. While you are worshiping God in a gathering of believers, keep your mind and spirit open to the Holy Spirit. Frequently, you will sense beforehand that there is going to be an utterance in tongues and that God is giving you the interpretation for it.

When that utterance comes, wait quietly until it is concluded. Initially, when you first begin to speak, you may only have the first sentence of the interpretation and a brief idea of what is to follow. Like all other gifts of the Spirit, this one operates by faith, too. As you commence to give forth what the Spirit is giving you, speak in a normal, clear, audible voice.

Strenuously avoid letting any personal thoughts, feelings, or ideas creep into the interpretation. Let your own thoughts be in neutral, and your mind be a clear channel for the Holy Spirit to flow through.

When the interpretation is complete and you sense that the Spirit has finished all He wishes to say, then stop!

Having delivered the interpretation, keep quiet while it is judged by those who sit by. If there are any believers present who are regularly used in the vocal gifts, they should judge whether the words are truly from God. The standard by which one may judge is similar to that which we would use for judging prophecy which is the next manifestation we will consider.

Discussion Question: If you have ever been given the gift of interpretation, following an utterance in tongues, share your experience with others.

Personal Application:

(1) Are you willing to let the Holy Spirit use you in public ministry by the gifts of the Spirit?
(2) Are you willing to abide by Paul's guidelines and have the interpretation given by you be judged by the mature believers in your church?

Memory Work

"Now there are diversities of gifts, but the same Spirit. And there are differences of administrations, but the same Lord. And there are diversities of operations, but it is the same God which worketh all in all. But the manifestation of the Spirit is given to every man to profit withal" (1 Cor. 12:4-7).

Lesson Seven

The Gift of Prophecy

Introduction

This week we are going to study the third vocal gift of the Spirit—prophecy. The gift of prophecy conveys the mind of the Lord to the church. The prophet speaks on behalf of God to believers.

Simply translated the word *prophesy* means "to utter inspired words. The purpose of prophecy is threefold:

- To edify the Church, build up and strengthen the believers
- To exhort them, stir them up, confront and challenge them
- To comfort and speak encouragingly

Oftentimes a prophecy may include all three of these elements.

Prayer: Lord, I know that spiritual things can never be understood by the natural mind, so by Your Holy Spirit, help me to understand these things of the Spirit. I thank You for the answer to this prayer. Amen.

Bible Study

Read **1 Corinthians 14:29-33.**

(1) Who may prophesy?

_____

(2) How many may prophesy at a meeting?

_____

(3) What should the others do?

_____

(4) Explain this scripture: "The spirits of the prophets are subject to prophets."

_____

_____

As we said before concerning speaking in tongues, the person speaking, though inspired by the Holy Spirit, is doing the actual speaking. God will not force him to speak.

Three misunderstandings about prophecy

A. Prophecy should not be confused with preaching.

Many today insist that the gift of prophecy is the ability to preach well. However, preaching and teaching are usually the result of prayerful meditation in the Word of God and careful preparation of one's mind and spirit in order to minister understanding to the people. In contrast, the gift of prophecy is not the result of careful study. It is a spontaneous speaking forth by the Spirit.

B. The gift of prophecy is not for foretelling the future.

This gift is for *forthtelling* rather than *foretelling*. Its purpose is for edification, exhortation and comfort and not for seeking to predict future events. Whenever there is an element of prediction within a prophecy, it is usually there because there is another gift (e.g. the word of knowledge or wisdom) working along with it.

C. This gift is not for personal guidance.

If we are in need of personal guidance, we should ask Jesus Himself for it (Jas. 1:5). If a prophetic utterance comes to us with instructions for the future, it should only be to confirm what God has already shown us personally.

Scriptural teaching about prophecy

Let us see now what the Bible has to say specifically about this wonderful gift God bestows upon us.

Read **1 Corinthians 14:3.**

(5) How does this verse describe the gift of prophecy?

_____

_____

(6) Using a dictionary, write out definitions of these three words:

edification _____

exhortation _____

comfort _____

Discussion Questions: Can you share a time when you have been edified, exhorted or consoled through someone using the gift of prophecy? What was your response?

Read **1 Corinthians 14:24,25.**

(7) What effect can prophecy have on the unbeliever?

_____

_____

_____

_____

Read **1 Corinthians 14:31.**
(8)   What effect can prophecy have on the believer?

_____

_____

This does not refer to the teaching which normally comes from the exposition of the Word of God through the ministry of a teacher. Rather, it is the learning of spiritual truths through the anointing of the Spirit. Such teachings should be tested by the written Word of God before being digested.

Read **1 Corinthians 14:1,39.**
(9)   What should be our attitude toward receiving the gift of prophecy?

_____

By the gift of prophecy we may be used of God for the encouragement of His people.

We have already learned that the person operating the gift is responsible for its use or abuse. Prophecy is not an uncontrolled utterance nor is the prophet under any kind of trance or mind control. Neither is he doing anything against his will. The spirit of prophecy is subject to the prophet. It is the prophet who is speaking, on behalf of God, and the prophet has control at all times of all that he or she is saying.

Characteristics of a genuine, Spirit-inspired prophecy

All prophecy should be judged. Here are some guidelines by which it can be judged.

- It will never contradict the written Word of God. Therefore, every prophetic utterance should be tested by the Word of God. God would never tell you by prophesy to do anything which His Word forbids.
- It will always exalt Jesus Christ, and never denigrate Him.
- It will edify, exhort and comfort the believers. It should never leave them confused, distressed, uncertain.
- It should "witness" with the majority of believers present (especially the more mature ones who are themselves frequently used in operation of vocal gifts).
- It will not break the spirit of the meeting, although it may change the course of it.

42

Read **Matthew 7:16.**
(10) How did Jesus say we could know false prophets?

_____

We should reject any so-called prophecy coming from one whose life
and practice are a reproach to the cause of Christ. Ultimately, the final
test of any predictive aspect of the prophecy is whether or not it comes
true.

Here are some guidelines for prophesying.
- Be relaxed. Don't be under a strain.
- Quietly wait upon the Lord in your spirit. Keep your mind open to
  His voice.
- When you feel the prompting of the Spirit within your spirit, com-
  mit yourself to God afresh as a channel for Him to flow through.
- Remember that the gift operates by faith.
- Begin to speak out whatever God gives you. Keep it simple.
- While you are speaking, be waiting upon the Lord quietly for the
  remainder of the message.
- Discern when the Spirit has finished speaking, and stop.

Read **Romans 12:6.**
(11) What are the limitations of our ability to prophesy?

_____

Personal Application:

(1) Do I honestly desire God's spiritual gifts?
(2) Am I willing to use them for the edification of the whole church? If
       not, am I willing to be made willing?

Memory Work

_"But if all prophesy, and there come in one that believeth not, or one un-
learned, he is convinced of all, he is judged by all: And thus are the
secrets of his heart made manifest; and so falling down on his face he will
worship God, and report that God is in you of a truth" (1 Cor. 14:24,25).
"For ye may all prophesy one by one, that all may learn, and all may be
comforted" (1 Cor. 14:31)._

Lesson Eight

The Gifts of Revelation

Introduction

We are now ready to take a look at the three revelation gifts. These are a word of knowledge, a word of wisdom and the discerning of spirits.

Prayer: Oh, God, how we need Your knowledge, Your wisdom, and Your discernment. Teach us everything You want us to know about these three precious gifts.

Bible Study

A word of knowledge

A word of knowledge is a fragment or small portion of God's knowledge containing certain facts and information through the supernatural revelation of the Holy Spirit. Supernaturally imparted, this information was previously unknown to the person and the knowledlge could not have been gained by any natural means.

We see Jesus using the word of knowledge in His ministry.

Read **John 1:47-50.**

(1) These verses record Jesus' first meeting with Nathaniel, who later became one of the twelve disciples. What did Jesus say to him?

_____

(2) How do we know that Jesus had not previously met Nathaniel?

_____

(3) What was Jesus' response?

_____

_____

The fig trees that grow in that area have extremely large leaves, not only covering the tree but the surrounding ground as well. Someone sitting under such a tree would be completely hidden from sight. Nathaniel knew that there was no way in the natural that Jesus could have seen him under the tree.

(4) What was Nathaniel's startled response?

_____

Read **John 4:18-20.**

This is the story of Jesus' encounter with the Samaritan woman at the well.

(5) What things about herself did Jesus tell her?

_____

_____

Read **John 4:28-30.**
(6) What did she say about Jesus to the villagers?

_____

_____

Jesus knew many facts about the woman of Samaria although He had never previously seen her. She was amazed by the accuracy of His knowledge concerning her past and present life. The exercise of the word of knowledge eventually brought about a real revival in Samaria.

The early Church also used the word of knowledge.

Read **Acts 9:10-16.**
(7) What did the Lord reveal about Paul to Ananias?

_____

_____

_____

_____

_____

Looking back to the Old Testament, we see certain people being given the word of knowledge.

Read **2 Samuel 12:1-14.**
(8) What did Nathan supernaturally know about David?

_____

_____

_____

Discussion Question: Can you think of other instances in the Bible where someone was given or used the word of knowledge?

Personal Question: Can you remember a time when (even if you did not recognize it for what it was) you were given a word of knowledge about someone?

Distinctions

A word of knowledge is distinct from human knowledge gained by natural means.
- It is not merely human knowledge sanctified by God.
- It cannot be gained by intellectual learning, by studying books or pursuing an academic course in a college or university.
- It is not the ability to study, understand or interpret the Bible.

Its employment in Scripture

Why does God give us the word of knowledge? Let's look to Scripture and see how it was used there.

(9) Write out how the word of knowledge was used in each of the following scriptures:

Acts 5:1-11 _____

John 1:47-50 _____

Acts 9:11 _____

John 11:11-15 _____

The operation of this gift
- It is supernatural in character—not obtained by logic or deduction, reasoning, etc., nor by the natural senses, but by supernatural revelation through the Holy Spirit.
- It operates by faith. The person receiving the revelation does so by faith. The revelation is received in one's spirit—not in the intellect or the emotions.
- It is not essentially a vocal gift. It is received quietly and inaudibly within the person's spirit.
- It may become vocal when shared with others (John 1:47, 4:18).

- Any Spirit-filled Christian who is willing to listen to God may experience the function of this gift.
- It is an invaluable asset in the ministry of counseling.
- Obedient action and response is essential to the continuing function of this manifestation of one's ministry.

It is frequently manifested in conjunction with the word of wisdom.

A word of wisdom

The word of wisdom is a fragment of divine wisdom supernaturally imparted by the Holy Spirit. It supplies one with the immediate wisdom to know what to say or do in a given situation.

This gift stands at the head of the list because it is so important. It enables us to speak and act with divine wisdom and thus ensures the correct use and application of the other gifts. When the word of wisdom is absent, the other gifts can be used incorrectly, causing much confusion.

As we have said before, God frequently gives the word of wisdom together with the word of knowledge, so that believers can know how to apply that word of knowledge correctly. Through a word of knowledge, God revealed to Ananias, the whereabouts and condition of Saul. He also showed him, by the word of wisdom, what he should do in this difficult situation.

Notice that it is a *word* (logos) of wisdom, and *not* the gift of wisdom. Let us give you an illustration.

Illustration

A man gets into legal difficulties and consults his lawyer. The lawyer does not give his client all the wisdom and knowledge he has. He extracts the word, or portion of his knowledge that applies to his client's needs and imparts that word. Likewise, God, who knows all things, extracts from His infinite store of wisdom, the particular portion of wisdom needed for one of His children. He sends this by the Holy Spirit.

What the word of wisdom is
- It is supernatural in character.
- It is given as the Holy Spirit wills (1 Cor. 12:11).
- It is given for a specific need or situation.

What the word of wisdom is not
- It is not natural wisdom.
- It is not the wisdom gained from academic achievement.
- It is not wisdom gained from experience.
- It is not even the wisdom to understand the Bible.

Biblical example

Read **Luke 4:1-13.**

(10) When Jesus was tempted in the wilderness, what were His answers to Satan?

_____

_____

_____

_____

How does anyone know how to respond to Satan's temptations? Today, we have Jesus' example, but the words of wisdom with which Jesus confronted Satan were imparted to Him by the Holy Spirit.

Read **Luke 20:22-26.**
(11) What was the word of wisdom the Holy Spirit gave to Jesus when the scribes tried to trap Him?

_____

_____

(12) What was their response?

_____

Read **John 8:3-11.**
(13) What is the situation?

_____

_____

(14) What is their motive?

_____

(15) How did Jesus handle the situation through the word of wisdom?

_____

_____

(16) What effect did this word of wisdom have on the Scribes and Pharisees?

_____

_____